AWESOME RIDDLES for Kids

ARCTURUS

This edition published in 2024 by Arcturus Publishing Limited
26/27 Bickels Yard, 151–153 Bermondsey Street,
London SE1 3HA

Illustrator: Chuck Whelon
Editors: Samantha Hilton and Joe Harris, with Julia Adams
Designer: Lucy Doncaster
Cover Designer: Amy McSimpson
Managing Editor: Joe Harris
Design Manager: Jessica Holliland

Published and Distributed in India by
Scholastic India Pvt. Ltd.
This reprint edition: February, 2025

ISBN: 978-93-5954-073-3

Printed in India at MicroPrints India, New Delhi

Contents

Did you hear about the joke book that was covered in glue?
You couldn't put it down!
Don't worry, there's no glue in this one—well, hardly any ...

Out and About!

Knock, knock.

Who's there?

Ken.

Ken who?

Ken I come in? It's freezing out here!

What do you use to cut the ocean in two?

A seasaw!

Where do sheep go on vacation?

The Baa-hamas!

What do you call a man with a car on his head?

Jack!

Riddle me this!

I keep running and running, but I never get tired. What am I?

A river.

Which U.S. state is round at each end and high in the middle?

Ohio!

Did you hear about the ship carrying blue paint that crashed into a ship carrying red paint?

The crews were marooned!

What are the only notes a pirate can sing?

High Cs!

What vegetable do sailors hate?

Leeks!

Riddle me this!

I fall at the North Pole, but I never get hurt. What am I?

Snow.

Try saying this three times, quickly.

She sells sea shells by the seashore!

What's brown, hairy, and wears sunglasses?

A coconut at the beach!

Did you hear about the commuter who chewed gum every morning?

He caught the chew-chew train!

Why did the pirate give his ship a coat of paint?

Because its timbers were shivering!

Knock, knock.

Who's there?

Canoe

Canoe who?

Canoe come out and play?

Say this three times, quickly.

The sixth sick sailor sat in the sinking ship!

What part of a car is the laziest?

The wheels, because they're always tired!

Try saying this three times, quickly.

The lucky crook took the cook's truck!

I'll only go to work after you've fired me. What am I?

A rocket!

How do lighthouse keepers communicate with each other?

With shine language!

What did the sailor think as he fell overboard?

Water way to go!

What did the toad say to the hitchhiking frog?

"Hop in!"

How do you annoy a pirate?

Take away the "p" to make him irate!

What do you get if you cross a dog and a plane

A jet-setter!

What did the sea captain say to the pilot after takeoff?

"This is plane sailing!"

Where do sharks go for a weekend break?

Fin-land!

Why did the spy get arrested at the station?

He was trying to cover his tracks!

What snakes do you find on cars?

Windshield vipers!

When is a car like a frog?

When it's being toad!

Try saying this three times, quickly.

Can a toucan canoe in the Yukon?

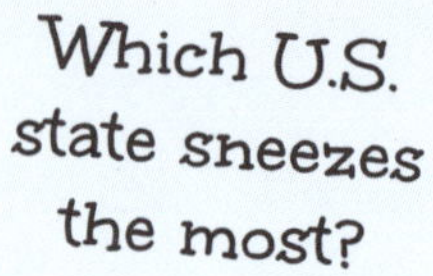

Which U.S. state sneezes the most?

Mass-achoo-setts!

Did you hear about the sick bicycle?

It was bed-ridden!

Why did the sailor cross the road?

To get to the other tide!

Why did the pirate leave a chicken with his buried treasure?

Because eggs marks the spot!

What is fluffy and green?

A seasick sheep!

Why is it hard to find a camel in the desert?

Because they're well camel-flaged!

Riddle me this!

I jump when I walk and sit when I stand. What am I?

A kangaroo.

What do you call a sleepy bull?

A bulldozer!

Why couldn't the astronaut land on the moon?

Because it was full!

What do you call a pirate with three eyes?

A piiirate!

How do you throw a space party?

You planet!

Did you hear about the frog that parked illegally?

It got toad away!

Try saying this three times, quickly.

Jumping jaguars juggle in the jungle!

Can you name five animals found at the North Pole?

Four seals and a polar bear!

How do pirates communicate with each other?

They use "Aye, aye!" phones!

What's fruity and purple and found off the coast of Australia?

The Grape Barrier Reef!

How do elephants travel long distances?

In jumbo jets!

What shoes should you wear when taking the train?

Platform shoes!

If there are ten cats on a train and one gets off, how many are left?

None—they're all copycats!

What do sailors like in their soup?

Crew-tons!

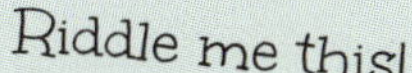

Riddle me this!

I'm not a tree, but I grow branches on my head. What am I?

A deer.

What do you call a camel without a hump?

Humphrey!

How did the hairdresser win the cycle race?

She took a shortcut!

What's big, scary, and has three wheels?

A T. rex riding a tricycle!

Which animal was the first in space?

The cow who jumped over the Moon!

What do you call a parrot that lives in a Mercedes?

A flying car-pet!

Riddle me this!

This key opens no doors, but you'll find it swinging through the jungle. What is it?

A monkey.

Why do seagulls live by the sea?

Because if they lived by the bay, they'd be bagels!

What is the hardest thing when you learn to ride a bike?

The ground!

What do you call a Frenchman wearing sandals?

Phillipe Flop!

Why should you never argue on a hot-air balloon ride?

You don't want to fall out!

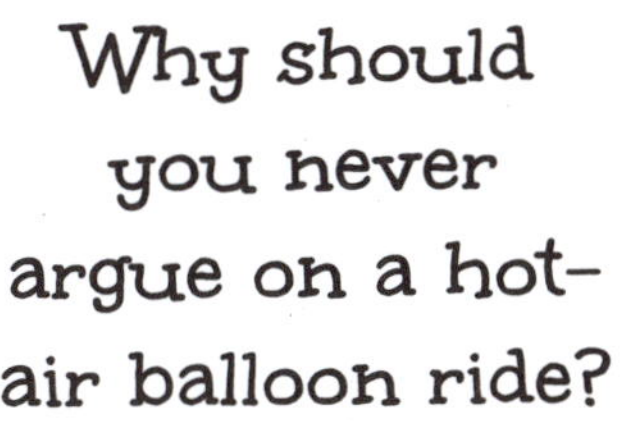

How do engines hear?

Through their engine-ears!

Where do pencils come from?

Pencil-vania!

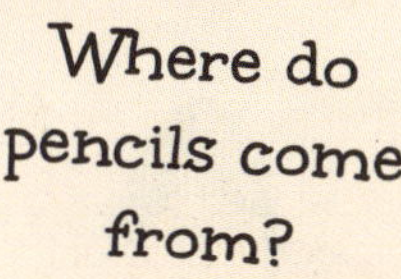

What did the four-by-four owner say in the blizzard?

"Snow problem!"

Riddle me this!

What do you call the streams that flow into the Nile?

Juveniles!

What do maps, fish, and music all have in common?

Scales.

Which is the fastest country in the world?

Rush-a!

How do fleas travel from place to place?

They itch-hike!

Say this three times, quickly.

It's terrifically tricky to trap twin tigers!

What do spiders study at art school?

Web design!

Knock, knock.

Who's there?

Mandy.

Mandy who?

Man, de traffic is terrible tonight!

Where do cows spend the night when they're away from home?

A moo-tel!

Why do bananas use sunscreen?

Because they peel!

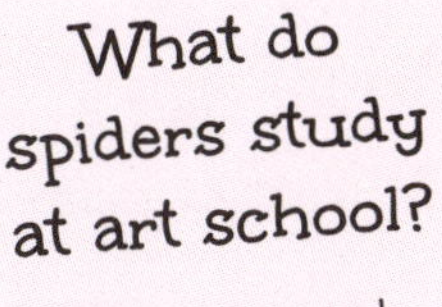

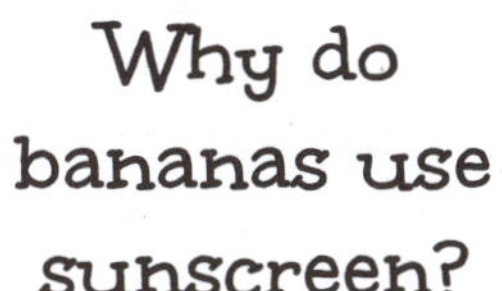

When is a sailor like a plank of wood?
When he's aboard!
Why are maps so bad at poker?
Because they always fold!
Which country is full of giant sea creatures?
Wales!
What do you call a train with a cold?
An achoo-choo train!

Knock, knock!

Who's there?

Joanna.

Joanna who?

Joanna go for a walk with me?

What did the fish say when it swam into the concrete wall?

"Dam!"

Who earns a living by driving their customers away?

A cab driver!

What's heavy, smelly, has four wheels, and flies?

A garbage truck on a hot summer's day!

What did one flag say to the other?

Nothing, it just waved!

What kind of hairstyle do sailors have?

A crew cut!

What flower is like a country of automobiles?

A car-nation!

You will find me in the middle of nowhere. What am I?

The letter "h"!

What do you call a boomerang that doesn't come back?

A stick!

What has big ears, four legs, and a trunk?

A mouse with its luggage.

Riddle me this!

I'm a type of building, but I weigh very little. What am I?

A lighthouse.

What is big, round, furry, and flies?

A hot-air baboon!

Why did the snake cross the desert?

To get to the other ssssside!

What is the best day to go the beach?

Sun-day!

Say this three times, quickly.

The ten-ton train rattles through the tunnel!

What do you get if you meet a shark in the Arctic Ocean?

Frostbite!

What did the baby bicycle call its father?

Pop-cycle!

How do bees get to school?

They take the school buzz!

Why do ghosts visit the same places every year?

They like their old haunts best!

How do you get ice off a hot-air balloon?

Use a skyscraper!

Did you hear the joke about the little mountain?

It's hill-arious!

What do you call a man that blocks a river?

Adam!

What should you take to avoid seasickness?

Vitamin sea!

Which is the coldest country in the world?

Chile!

I am the strongest animal under the sea. What am I?

A mussel!

What does a houseboat want to be when it grows up?

A township!

Where do sailors keep their books?

On the continental shelf!

Why did the pirate visit the Apple store?

To buy an i-Patch!

If shoes are made from leather, what's made from bananas?

Slippers!

What do Inuit people use to hold their houses together?

Ig-glue!

What goes MOOZ?

A spaceship reversing!

Why did the bridge get angry?

Because people were always crossing it!

Riddle me this!

I live in the sea, but I look like I'm from outer space. What am I?

A starfish.

Where do hamsters come from?

Hamsterdam!

Why did the farmer ride his horse into town?

Because it was too heavy to carry!

Why did the robot go on vacation?

He needed to recharge his batteries!

What do you need to drive your car underwater?

Four-eel drive!

Why do French people love to eat snails?

They don't like fast food!

Riddle me this!

A man went into town on Friday, stayed two nights, then went home on Friday. How?

His horse's name was Friday!

What's worse than raining cats and dogs?

Hailing taxis!

Did you hear about the cuddly sea captain?

He liked to hug the shore!

What kind of music do astronauts like?

Rocket and roll!

What was the highest mountain before Everest was discovered?

Still Mount Everest!

Say this three times, quickly.

The ship's chef's sushi made Suzie seasick!

Silly Ever After

What happened to the wizard who skipped school?

He was ex-spelled!

Why don't bad-tempered witches ride broomsticks?

In case they fly off the handle!

Why did Little Miss Muffet need a map?

Because she'd lost her whey!

Why should you never sleep with your head under the pillow?

Because the tooth fairy might take all your teeth!

What do sea monsters eat?

Fish and ships!

Did you hear about the witches who were identical twins?

You couldn't tell which witch was which!

Try saying this three times, quickly.

This witch wishes to switch wands!

This magically turns everything round without moving. What is it?

A mirror

What's the first thing a witch reads in a magazine?

Her horror-scope!

Try saying this three times, quickly!

If two witches were watching two watches, which witch would watch which watch?

Why was Cinderella thrown off the football team?

Because she kept running away from the ball!

What did the mermaid keep as a pet?

A catfish!

Why do dragons lay eggs?

Because if they dropped them, they would break!

Which North American lake is popular with witches?

Lake Eerie!

Try saying this three times, quickly.

Glowing, green globes glisten in the gloom.

What does a wizard put on his hair?

Scare gel!

Why don't witches wear top hats?

Because there's no point!

What do you get when you cross a witch with a dinosaur?

A Tyrannosaurus hex!

Did you hear about the wizard who turned himself into a frog?

He's still hopping mad about it!

Knock, knock.

Who's there?

Witches.

Witches who?

Witches the way to the Monster's Ball?

Why didn't the mermaid warn her daughter about the electric eel?

It was too shocking!

Why did the mermaid blush?

Because she saw the bottom of the ocean!

Who keeps the ocean floor clean?

The mermaids!

Try saying this three times, quickly.

Dwayne the dwarf drew Dracula's weird dragon!

Did you hear about the vampire who loved baseball?

He kept turning into a bat!

Knock, knock.

Who's there?

Ivana.

Ivana who?

Ivana suck your blood!

Where do ogres like to go shopping?

The gross-ery store!

What did the fairy name her daughter?

Wanda!

Riddle me this!

What has a head and a tail but no body?

A coin.

What did the witch say to the black cat?

"You seem familiar!"

What is a witch's best subject at school?

Spelling!

Why did the silly boy carry a cuckoo clock on Halloween?

He'd heard it was tick or tweet!

What do you say when you meet a werewolf?

"Howl do you do?"

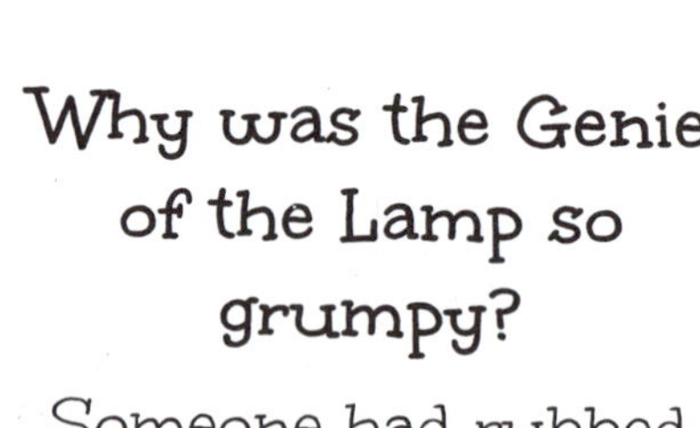

Why was the Genie of the Lamp so grumpy?

Someone had rubbed him up the wrong way!

What does Cinderella wear underwater?

Glass flippers!

Why do witches love hotels?

They can order broom service!

How does an octopus make a mermaid laugh?

With ten-tickles!

Riddle me this!

I have a face and two hands but no arms or legs. What am I?

A clock.

Try saying this three times, quickly.

Trixie picks pink pansies for pixies!

What type of dog does dracula have?

A bloodhound!

Why was the witch late for school?

Because she overswept!

Knock, knock.

Who's there?

Ice cream.

Ice cream who?

Ice cream if you don't let me in!

What's the difference between a unicorn and a carrot?

One is a funny beast, and the other is a bunny feast!

How do you make a witch itch?

Take away the "w"!

Why didn't the pixie invite his school friend over for supper?

His mother couldn't stand the goblin!

What do you give an ogre with enormous feet?

Plenty of room!

What do you call a petunia that goes to magic school?

Harry Potplant!

How does an ogre count to twelve?

On his fingers!

Riddle me this!

I have thirteen hearts but no brains. What am I?

A deck of cards.

What do ghosts like to eat for dessert?

I scream!

Where do witches leave their children while they're at work?

Dayscare!

How do you know when a magician has lost his temper?

He pulls his hare out!

Why does Peter Pan fly everywhere?

He Neverlands!

Try saying this three times, quickly!

The cute Quidditch kids quit the Quidditch pitch quite quietly.

Who goes out with an ogre?

His girlfiend!

What is taller than a giant?

A giant's hat!

Knock, knock.

Who's there?

Ogre.

Ogre who?

O gr-eat, you're at home!

Try saying this three times, quickly.

Gargling gargoyles gobble gross goblins greedily!

Did you hear about the ugly Cyclops?

He was a sight for a sore eye!

Where do you find giant snails?

On a giant's fingers!

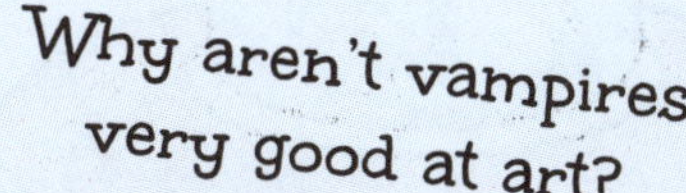

Why aren't vampires very good at art?

Because they can only draw blood!

What kind of books do magicians' rabbits like?

Ones with hoppy endings!

How do mermaids like their hair?

Wavy!

Why did the wizard fail his exam?

He was terrible at spelling!

Why are witches' hotel bills so high.

They always ask for broom service.

What do you call a wizard from outer space?

A flying sorcerer!

What did the skeleton order for dinner?

Spare ribs!

Knock, knock.

Who's there?

Boo.

Boo who?

No need to cry, I'm just trick or treating!

What kind of witch is useful when it's dark?

A lights-witch!

What do you call a haunted chicken?

A poultry-geist!

Try saying this three times, quickly.

The wizard winked wickedly while waving his wand!

Knock, knock.

Who's there?

Tinker bell.

Tinker bell who?

I tinker bell is out of order!

You'll never find any ghosts in this room. Which room am I?

The living room.

Why did Dopey the dwarf stare at the orange juice carton for hours?

Because the label said "Concentrate"!

Who is Aladdin's smartest friend?

The genie-us of the lamp!

Why did the octopus annoy the mermaid?

He was always squidding around!

Say this three times, quickly.

The green goblins greedily gobbled their gooey goodies!

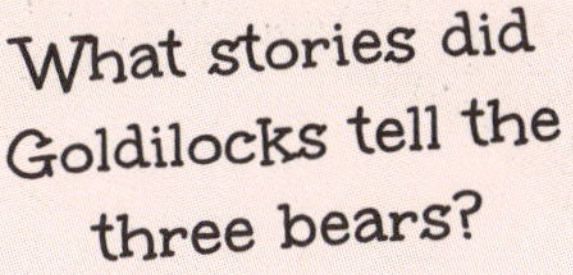

What stories did Goldilocks tell the three bears?

Furry tales!

How do mermaids do their shopping?

They surf the net!

Why should you never trust the big bad wolf when he's in bed?

Because he's lying!

Where do you find giant armies?

In a giant's sleevies!

What do you call a skeleton who won't work?

Lazy bones!

Knock, knock.

Who's there?

Frank.

Frank who?

Frankenstein.

What position does a ghost play in soccer?

Ghoulie!

Say this three times, quickly.

Eleven elves ate enchanted eggs in an elm tree!

What do witches always eat at Halloween?

Ghoulash!

Where do the toughest dragons come from?

Hard-boiled eggs!

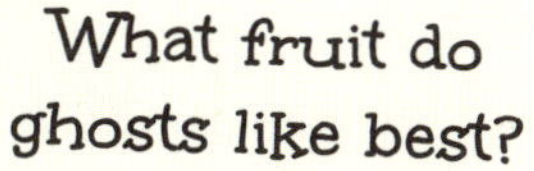

What fruit do ghosts like best?

Boo-berries!

Why did the skeleton stay at home?

Because he had no body to go out with!

Why didn't the mummy have any friends?

Because he was too wrapped up in himself!

Why didn't the zombie go to school?

Because he felt rotten!

Why doesn't Harry Potter's godfather like practical jokes?

He's always Sirius!

What do French skeletons say before dinner?

"Bone appetit!"

Riddle me this!

How do you make the number one disappear?

Add the letter "G" and it's "GONE"!

What is at the end of a rainbow?

The letter "w"!

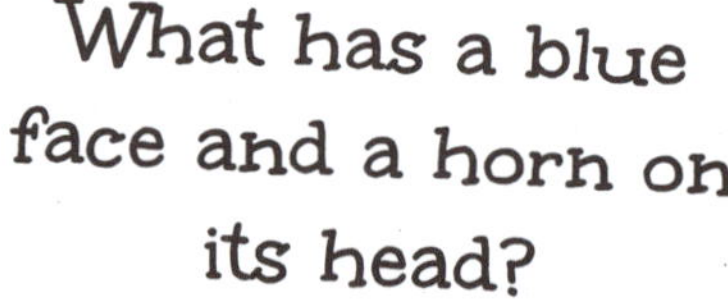

What has a blue face and a horn on its head?

A unicorn holding its breath!

What do you get if you take a bunch of witches to the beach?

A pile of sand-witches!

Why are ghosts so bad at lying?

Because you can see right through them!

What game do vampires love to play?

Casket-ball!

Riddle me this!

I have an eye, but I cannot see. What am I?

A needle.

Why don't ghosts like the rain?

It dampens their spirits!

Where does Count Dracula keep his money?

In a blood bank!

What happened when two banshees met each other at a party?

It was love at first fright!

What do vampires do at the end of the school year?

Blood tests!

Riddle me this!

You'll never see us by daylight, although there are billions of us. What are we?

Stars.

How did Jack figure out how many beans his cow was worth?

He used a cow-culator!

What do you call a one-eyed creature riding a BMX?

A bicyclops!

What's purple and screams from the top of a tower?

A damson in distress!

Did you hear about the magician who threw his watch up in the air?

He wanted to see time fly!

Say this three times, quickly.

Sixty pesky pixies pestered poor Peter!

How do we know Rapunzel liked to party?

Because she always let her hair down!

What do you call a creature that gets lost when there's a full moon?

A where-wolf!

What do you do with a green monster?

Wait until it's ripe!

Why do witches fly on brooms?

Because vacuum cleaners are too heavy!

Riddle me this!

Just one shade but changing size. Present in sunlight but gone at night!

What am I?

A shadow.

Knock, knock.

Who's there?

Jacklyn.

Jacklyn who?

Jacklyn Hyde!

What do witches spread on their bread?

Scream cheese!

Did you hear the gloomy story about the bear?

It was a grim, furry tale!

Why don't bats live alone?

They like hanging out with their friends!

Say this three times, quickly.

Which wicked witch wished the wicked wish?

How can you tell if a banshee is polite?

She only shrieks when she's spoken to!

Knock, knock.

Who's there?

Fifi.

Fifi who?

Fifi, fiefie, fofo, fum, I smell the blood of an Englishman!

Why can't you borrow money from a leprechaun?

They're always a little short!

What is the first thing pixies learn at school?

The elf-abet!

Why do dragons sleep during the day?

So they can fight knights!

What has sharp teeth and lives at the end of the rainbow?

The croc of gold!

Weird World

Did you hear about the snakes that argued?

They agreed to hiss and make up!

What did the tornado say to the plane?

"Want to go for a spin?"

How do snails keep their shells so shiny?

They use snail polish!

Say this three times, quickly.

Many mini mice make marvellous merry music.

What is on top of a snowman's bed?

A blanket of snow!

What do you call a funny chicken?

A comedi-hen!

What did the cloud say to the bolt of lightning?

"You're shocking!"

What did the worm say to her son when he came home late?

"Where in earth have you been?"

What kind of clothes do storm clouds wear?

Thunderwear!

Where do fish keep their money?

In the riverbank!

What part of the ocean is the deepest?

The bottom!

A pony went to see the doctor because it had a sore throat.

"I know what's wrong," said the doctor. "You're a little horse!"

Why couldn't the snake say anything?

It had a frog in its throat!

What do horses wear at the beach?

Clip-clops!

How can you tell that a cat likes the rain?

Because when it rains, it purrs!

Why aren't trees good at quizzes?

Because they're often stumped!

Riddle me this!

I often drop, but I never hit the ground. What am I?

The temperature.

Did you hear about the silkworms that had a race?

They ended up in a tie!

Why is it hard to tease a snake?

You can't pull its leg!

Riddle me this!

What is the largest moth in the world?

A mammoth.

What's black and white and red all over?

A sunburned penguin!

What do cows do when they visit New York?

They go to see a moosical!

What kind of tree can fit into your hand?

A palm tree!

Try saying this three times, quickly.

Six silver swans swam silently seaward!

What dog loves to take bubble baths?

A shampoodle!

Knock, knock.

Who's there?

Cowsgo.

Cowsgo who?

No, they don't. Cows go moo!

Did you hear about the bee born in the spring?

Maybee...

What musical instrument are fish afraid of?

Casta-nets!

How do trees access the Internet?

They log in.

Why shouldn't you tell jokes in the Arctic?

The ice might crack up!

This animal wears a coat in winter, but in summer, it wears a coat and pants. What is it?

A dog!

Why do male deer need to wear braces?

Because they have buck teeth!

What did the duck say after he went shopping?

"Put it on my bill!"

Which sea creature eats its prey two at a time?

Noah's shark!

Which animals are caterpillars most afraid of?

Dog-erpillars!

Why don't oysters share their pearls?

Because they're shellfish!

What did the vet give the sick horse?

Cough stirrup!

What's worse than finding a worm in your apple?

Finding half a worm in your apple!

Say this three times, quickly.

I think extinct insects stink!

Why do penguins carry fish in their beaks?

Because they don't have any pockets!

What kind of pigs know karate?

Pork chops!

Why don't oysters like loud music?

Because a noisy noise annoys an oyster!

What game do tornadoes play?

Twister!

Say this three times, quickly.

The six, sick, slimy snails sailed silently!

What do you call a mackerel in a tuxedo?

So-fish-ticated!

What do you call an ambitious wasp?

A wanna-bee!

What happened to the snowman in the spring?

He made a pool of himself!

What sound do porcupines make when they kiss?

Ouch!

What do you call a deer with no eyes?

No idea!

Say this three times, quickly.

A big, black bug blew big, blue bubbles!

What do you call a snake that works for the government?

A civil serpent!

What do polar bears eat for lunch?

Iceberg-ers!

Why are dolphins so clever?

Because they swim in schools!

What do acorns learn at school?

Their tree times table!

What kind of animal will never oversleep?

A llama clock!

What did the crab say to her grouchy husband?

"Don't get snappy with me!"

Say this three times, quickly.

If you go for a gopher, the gopher will go for a hole!

Cross a frog with a flower and this is what you get.

A croak-us!

Why does the Moon wear sunglasses?

Because it's way cooler than the Sun!

What do you call a baby crab?

A little nipper!

What did one raindrop say to the other?

"Two's company, three's a cloud!"

How do you stop a rhino from charging?

Unplug it!

Why don't owls date during thunderstorms?

It's too wet to woo!

Why wasn't the octopus afraid of being attacked?

It was well armed!

How many of each animal did Moses take on the ark?

None. Noah built the ark, not Moses!

Why did the vultures argue?

They had a bone to pick with each other!

Say this three times, quickly.

How much wood would a woodchuck chuck, if a woodchuck could chuck wood?

What's the best season to buy a trampoline?

Spring!

Why can't a leopard hide?

Because he's always spotted!

Riddle me this!

Go ahead and slice me apart ... you'll be the one crying! What am I?

An onion.

What is in the middle of a jellyfish?

Its jelly button!

What is the biggest ant in the world?

The eleph-ant!

What lives in the forest and never stops talking?

A wild boar!

What does the Sun drink out of?

Sunglasses!

Why did the Sun go to school?

To get brighter!

Knock, knock.

Who's there?

Toucan.

Toucan who?

Toucan play that game!

Try saying this three times, quickly.

Felix fries fresh fish for Friday's fresh-fish festival!

What kind of animal is the best at breakdancing?

A hip-hop-potamus!

What do you get if you cross a frog with a flower?

A croak-us!

Did you hear about the happy raindrop?

It was on Cloud Nine!

What do you call a woman who is good at fishing?

Annette!

Say this three times, quickly.

Swedish sword-swallowers swallow swords swiftly!

Knock, knock.

Who's there?

Rhino.

Rhino who?

Rhino every knock, knock joke there is!

What are the silliest flowers in the garden?

Daffy-dils!

What is a snake's best subject?

Hiss-tory!

What do you call a bee that keeps falling over?

A stumble-bee!

Why don't fish ever win at poker?

Because of all the card sharks!

What did the tree do when the bank was closed?

It tried another branch!

How do you describe an acorn?

In a nutshell, it's an oak tree!

Riddle me this!

I'm an insect, and the first half of my name is another insect. What am I?

A beetle.

What do you call a rabbit with fleas?

Bugs bunny!

What do you call a bee that is unhappy?

A grumble-bee!

What did the bird say as it finished building its nest?

"That's the last straw!"

What do you call a man with pockets full of dry leaves?

Russell!

Riddle me this!

Feed me and I live, but give me a drink, and I die. What am I?

Fire.

What do you call a man with a seagull on his head?

Cliff!

What do you call a snake that builds houses?

A boa constructor!

What should you do in the presence of a mighty tree?

Take a bough!

What do trees wear to the pool?

Swimming trunks!

How do you get in touch with a fish?

You drop it a line!

Knock, knock.

Who's there?

Bat.

Bat who?

Bat you'll never guess!

Which animal can jump higher than a building?

All animals can ... because buildings can't jump!

Why do you call that reptile "Tiny"?

Because he's my newt!

Why didn't the viper wipe 'er nose?

Because the adder 'ad 'er 'andkerchief!

Say this three times, quickly.

Two tiny tigers took taxis into town!

What does a lion say when he's introduced at a party?

"Pleased to eat you!"

What's orange and sounds like a parrot?

A carrot!

What did the farmer say to the cow when she ran out of milk?

"You're an udder failure!"

What is a myth?

A female moth!

What do you get from a pampered cow?

Spoiled milk!

Cindy: It's really raining cats and dogs today.

Mindy: I know, I just stepped in a poodle!

Riddle me this!

I am most useful when I'm broken. What am I?

An egg.

What do you call a girl with a turtle on her head?

Shelley!

What month do lumberjacks like the best?

Sep-timber!

Say this three times, quickly.

How many clams can you cram in a clean cream can?

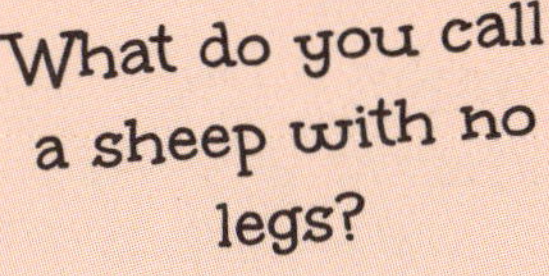

What do you call a sheep with no legs?

A cloud!

Who stole the soap?

The robber ducky!

What do you call a bear in wet weather?

A drizzly bear!

What game did the cat like to play with the mouse?

Catch!

What's full of holes but holds lots of water?

A sponge!

No matter how much it rains, I never get any wetter. What am I?

A lake.

How can you tell a worm's head from its tail?

Tickle the middle, and see which end laughs!

What type of bird works on a building site?

A crane!

What do you call a T. rex with magical powers?

A dino-sorcerer!

Say this three times, quickly.

Can a toucan do the cancan? Can two toucans do the cancan, too?

Laughter Starts at Home!

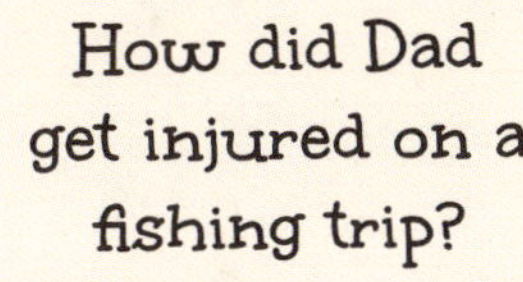

How did Dad get injured on a fishing trip?

He pulled a mussel!

Kurt: What has four legs, pimples, and smells bad?

Bert: Me and my brother!

Mother: Please can you help me fix dinner?

Daughter: Why, is it broken?

Did you hear that Uncle Bob lost his wig on the roller coaster?

It was a hair-raising experience!

Riddle me this!

I'm tall when I'm young but short when I'm old. What am I?

A candle.

Why was the octopus worried about her son?

Because he was a crazy, mixed-up squid!

Why did the woman go out of the house with her purse open?

She expected some change in the weather!

What did the mother dog say to the puppy?

"We're having dinner soon ... don't eat too much homework!"

Say this three times, quickly.

Simon's sister's socks sat in a sink soaking in soapsuds!

Riddle me this!

What goes up but never comes down?

Your age.

How do you define "cartoon"?

Music you listen to in the car!

Dad: Why have you been missing school, son?

Son: I haven't missed it one little bit!

What did the mother broom say to her son at bedtime?

"It's time to go to sweep!"

Knock, knock.

Who's there?

Anita.

Anita who?

Anita borrow a cup of sugar!

What do you get if you cross baked beans with onions?

Tear gas!

Raquel: Why does your dad wear two sweaters when he plays golf?

Michelle: In case he gets a hole in one!

Why did everyone laugh at the cowboy?

He was always horsing around!

What do you get if you cross Dad's socks with a boomerang?

A nasty smell that keeps coming back!

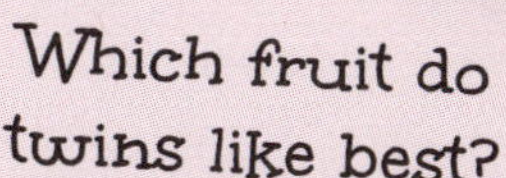

Which fruit do twins like best?

Pears!

Do robots have brothers?

No, but they do have transistors!

Why was the little iceberg just like his dad?

Because he was a chip off the cold block!

What do you do if you find a dinosaur in your bed?

Find somewhere else to sleep!

What kind of monster lives in your brother's room?

The Loch Mess Monster!

Knock, knock.

Who's there?

Dishes.

Dishes who?

Dish-es me, who are you?

What can you give and keep at the same time?

A cold!

My cousin is so dumb, he took his computer to the nurse because it had a virus!

Winnie: Why is there a plane outside your bedroom door?

Vinnie: I must have left the landing light on!

Say this three times, quickly.

If your dog chews shoes, whose shoes does he choose?

What did the Italian say when he returned from an overseas trip?

"Rome, sweet Rome!"

Why did the boy throw butter out of the window?

To see the butterfly!

Say this three times, quickly.

There's a kitten in mittens eating chicken in the kitchen!

David's father has three sons: Snap, Crackle, and...?

David!

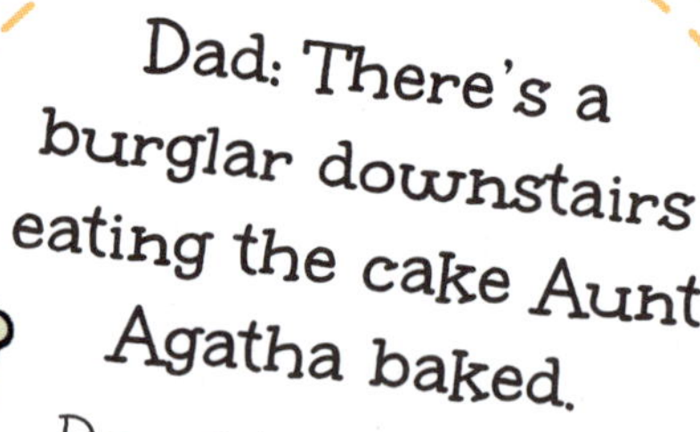

Dad: There's a burglar downstairs eating the cake Aunt Agatha baked.

Daughter: Should I call the police or an ambulance?

Why is your sister so good at sports?

She has athlete's foot!

My mother's excellent at history, but she's an awful cook.

She's an expert on ancient grease!

Kid: Can I have a canary for Christmas?

Dad: No, you'll have turkey, like everyone else!

What do you call a baby skunk?

A little squirt!

Why were the glowworms' parents so happy?

Because their children were all very bright!

What is stranger than seeing a cat fish?

Seeing a goldfish bowl!

Knock, knock.

Who's there?

Aunt.

Aunt who?

Aunt you gonna let me in?

Daughter: I can't mow the lawn today. I've twisted my ankle.

Mother: That's a lame excuse!

Why was the youngest of seven children late for school?

Because the alarm was set for six!

What should you do if a teenage monster rolls her eyes at you?

Roll them back to her!

Say this three times, quickly.

Will merry Murray marry Mary or Marie?

Why did the cat always hang out near the piano?

She was looking for the piano tuna!

Why did the house go to the hospital?

Because it had a windowpane!

What did the baby corn say to his mother?

"Where's Pop?"

Knock, knock.

Who's there?

Someone on a pogo stick.

Tell them to hop it!

What do you say to someone sitting on your roof?

"High there!"

I am a room with no walls. What am I?

A mushroom.

When should a mouse stay indoors?

When it's raining cats and dogs!

My dad can juggle eggshells, yesterday's newspaper, and an empty box!

That's garbage!

Knock, knock.

Who's there?

Lettuce.

Lettuce who?

Lettuce in! We're freezing!

What do you give to a baby snake?

A rattle!

Why shouldn't you worry if you see mice in your home?

They're probably doing the mouse-work!

"Son, why didn't you come straight home from school?"

"Because we live around the corner!"

Son: This fish has bones in it.

Mother: Are you choking?

Son: No, I'm serious!

Sandy: Can we watch *The Curse of the Black Pearl* tonight?

Mandy: No, Dad won't let us watch pirate DVDs!

Say this three times, quickly.

I like a proper cup of coffee from a proper copper coffee pot!

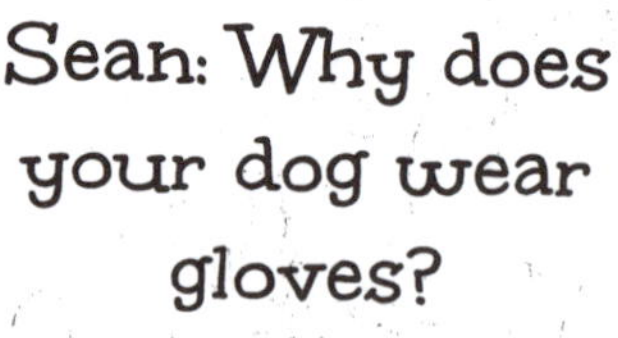

Sean: Why does your dog wear gloves?

Vaughn: It's a boxer!

Why are there more ghost cats than ghost dogs?

Because every cat has nine lives!

What Ancient Greek land is like your brother's bedroom?

Mess-opotamia!

Why is your brother running around his bed?

He's trying to catch up on his sleep!

What did the quilt say to the bed?

"I've got you covered!"

What did the cowboy say when his pet dog ran away?

"Well, doggone!"

My cousin is so dumb, he took toilet paper to the party in case of party poopers!

"Did your mother help you with your homework?"

"No, I got it wrong all by myself!"

"My dad had to go to court for stealing a calendar. You know what he got?"

"Twelve months!"

When is a basketball player like a baby?

When he dribbles!

What has many keys but cannot open a door?

A piano.

How did the dog feel after he ate the pillow?

Down in the mouth!

Who are small, furry, and fantastic at sword fighting?

The Three Mouseketeers!

What do you call x-rays taken by your dentist?

Tooth pics!

Why is your dog chasing its tail?

It's trying to make both ends meet!

What happened when Granny Smith married Mr. Braeburn?

They lived appley ever after!

Thelma: If that planet is Mars, what's the one higher up?

Velma: Is it Pa's?

What prize did the inventor of the door knocker win?

The No-bell Prize!

Knock, knock.

Who's there?

Little old lady.

Little old lady who?

Wow! I didn't know you could yodel!

Why are you eating that baguette in the bathtub?

It's a sub sandwich!

Did you hear about the embarrassing dads in the fathers' race?

One ran in short bursts, the other ran in burst shorts!

What happened when the invisible man married the invisible woman?

Their kids were nothing to look at!

What instrument do dogs like best?

The trom-bone!

Edwin: I don't like cheese with holes.

Dad: Well, eat the cheese, and leave the holes on the side of your plate!

Which relative visits astronauts in outer space?

Auntie Gravity!

Knock, knock.

Who's there?

Amit.

Amit who?

Amit your sister at the movies last night!

How do you know when there's an elephant under your bed?

Your nose is touching the ceiling!

Dan: My teacher says I should train to be an astronaut.

Anne: No, he said you're a real space cadet!

What did one toilet say to the other?

"You look flushed!"

How do you make antifreeze?

Hide her coat and gloves!

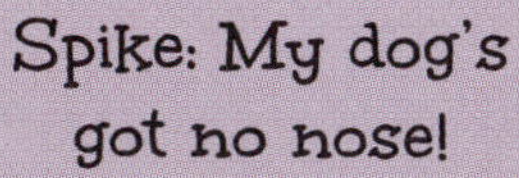

Spike: My dog's got no nose!

Mike: How does he smell?

Spike: Terrible!

My brother is so dumb, he found three milk cartons in a field and thought it was a cow's nest!

Riddle me this!

What belongs to you, even though other people use it more than you do?

Your name.

How do you warm up a room after it's been painted?

Give it a second coat!

What happened to the dog that swallowed a firefly?

Its spark was worse than its bite!

What do you give your pet rat to eat?

Ratatouille!

Why did the programmer sell his cat?

He thought it might eat his mouse!

I am as light as a feather, but no one can hold me for long. What am I?

Your breath.

Why was 6 scared of 7?

Because 7, 8, 9!

Why did the robber take a bath before he stole from the bank?

He wanted to make a clean getaway!

Teacher: What is the plural of baby?

Frances: Twins!

Say this three times, quickly.

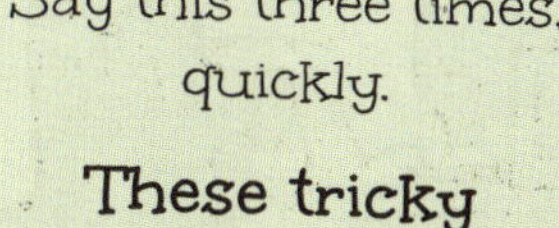

These tricky tongue twisters trip thrillingly off the tongue!

Why do dogs run in circles?

Because it's hard to run in squares!

Riddle me this!

I have one foot, one head, and four legs. What am I?

A bed.

"Dad, how can I join the police?"

"Handcuff them all together!"

What do a pet dog and a phone have in common?

They both have collar I.D.!

Why did the jogger eat on the run?

She loved fast food!

What did the mother cow say to her calf at night?

"It's pasture bedtime!"

What's the difference between a moaning parent and a boring book?

You can shut a book up!

Why was the baby panda so spoiled?

Because its mother panda-d to its every whim!

I go up and down but never move. What am I?

Stairs.

Annie: Why did your dad quit his job at the can-crushing plant?"

Danny: Because it was soda pressing!

Riddle me this!

What goes up when the rain comes down?

An umbrella.

How do you know carrots are good for your eyes?

Because you never see a rabbit wearing glasses!

Why are an old man's teeth like stars?

Because they come out at night!

What does a fashionable house wear?

Address!

What book do sharks read to their kids at bedtime?

Huckleberry Finn!

Why is the letter "A" most like a flower?

Because the "B" is after it!

What do cats put in their cola?

Mice cubes!

Ron: Why are you taking planks and a hammer to the gym?

John: I'm going for fencing lessons!

Why was the cat silent?

A person got its tongue!

What makes you say your brother is dumb?

He tried to borrow Facebook from the library!

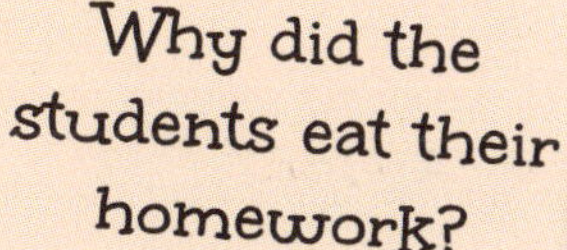

Why did the students eat their homework?

Because the teacher said that it was a piece of cake!

Why did the mushroom get invited to so many parties?

Because he was a fun guy!

What time is it when an elephant sits on your fence?

Time to get a new fence!

Little pencil: You look as though you've put on weight, Dad.

Daddy pencil: You're very blunt!

Knock, Knock.

Who's there?

Cash.

Cash who?

I knew you were a nut!

How can you spell something rotten with just two letters?

D.K.!

How many skunks does it take to stink up a house?

A phew!

Did you hear about the magician who tried his sawing-a-person-in-two tricks at home?

He had lots of half brothers and sisters!

Hilarious History

Where did Montezuma go to college?

Az Tech!

How did the Egyptian pharaoh get around?

In his mummy's car.

Who succeeded the first President of the United States?

The second one!

What do you call a sleeping Triceratops?

A dino-snore!

Why were the early days of history called the Dark Ages?

Because there were so many knights!

What was the first thing said by the inventor of the stink bomb?

"You reek, ugh!"

Say this three times, quickly.

Two terrible T. rex wreck trains together!

How did Vikings send secret messages?

They used Norse code!

Why does the Statue of Liberty stand outside New York?

It can't sit down!

What was Camelot famous for?

Its knight life!

Why did Eve want to move to New York?

She wanted to see the Big Apple!

Who built the ark?

I have Noah idea!

Which king invented fractions?

Henry the 1/8!

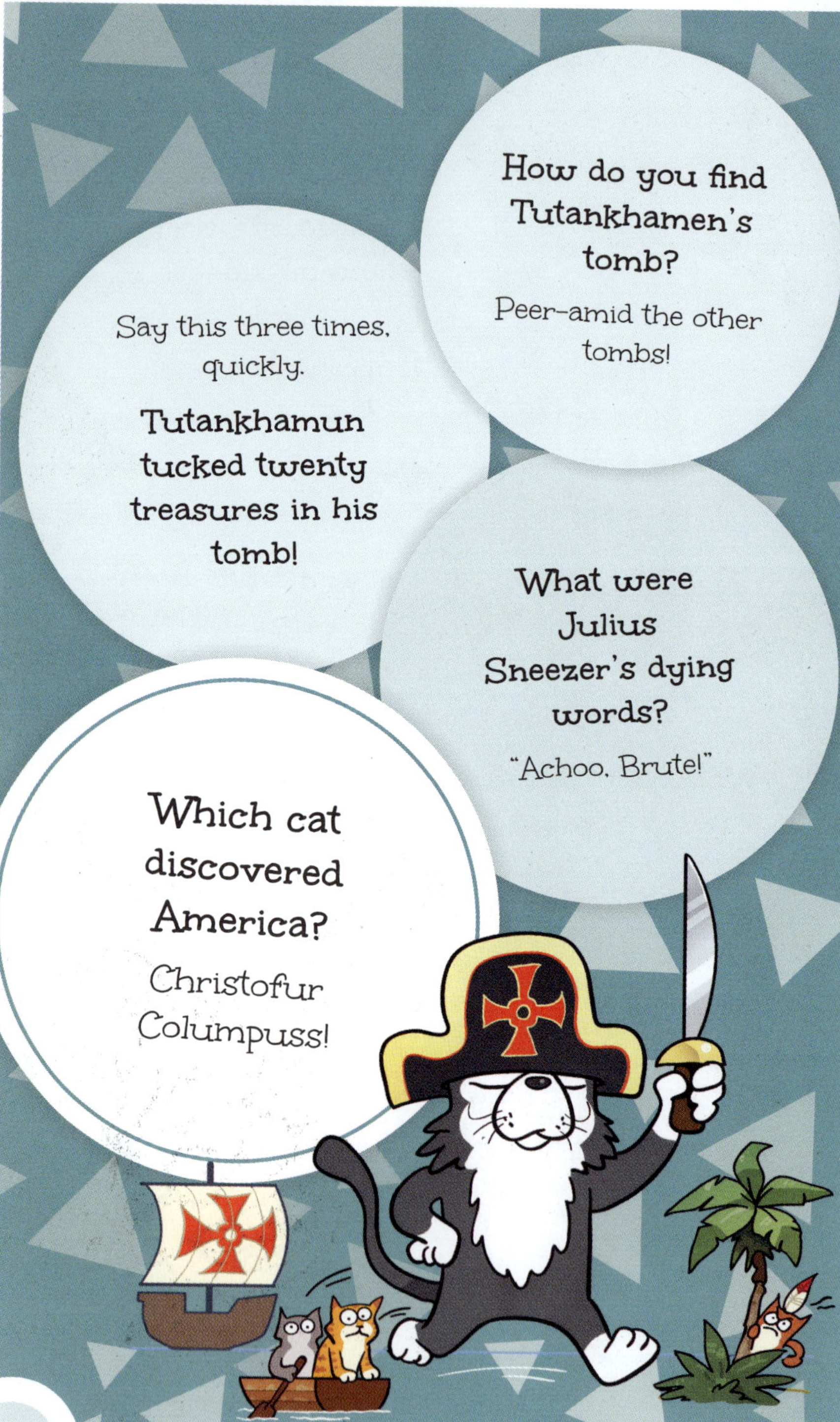
How do you find Tutankhamen's tomb?
Peer-amid the other tombs!
Say this three times, quickly.
Tutankhamun tucked twenty treasures in his tomb!
What were Julius Sneezer's dying words?
"Achoo, Brute!"
Which cat discovered America?
Christofur Columpuss!

Who was Wyatt Burp's best friend?

Wild Bill Hiccup!

Which ancient people moved around the most?

The Roam-ans!

What movie did the ancient Greeks like best?

Troy Story!

Why did everyone in nineteenth-century England carry an umbrella?

Because Queen Victoria's reign lasted for 64 years!

Knock, knock.

Who's there?

Robin.

Robin who?

Robin the rich to give to the poor!

What do you call a Roman emperor with a cold?

Julius Sneezer!

What invention lets you see through walls?

The window!

Why did Renoir become an Impressionist?

He did it for the Monet!

Which famous gunfighter had indigestion?

Wyatt Burp!

What happened to the royal chicken that couldn't lay eggs?

The king had her eggs-ecuted!

Need an ark to save two of every animal?

I Noah guy...

What do kings and queens drink at breakfast?

Royal-tea!

Did you hear about the card game on Noah's Ark?

It was ruined by a cheetah!

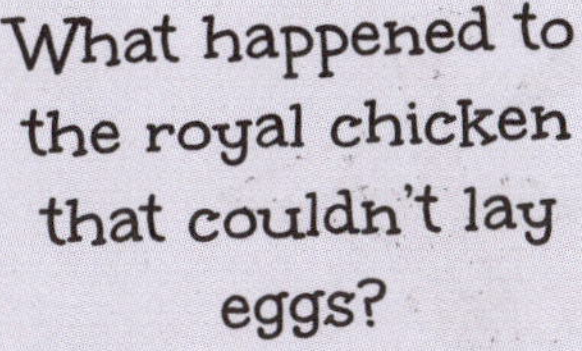

Which owl robbed the rich to give to the poor?

Robin Hoot!

What kind of king wears a horned crown?

A Vi-king!

What do history teachers talk about on dates?

The good old days!

What is the fruitiest subject at school?

History, because it's full of dates!

Why can't you hear a Pterodactyl going to the bathroom?

Because the "p" is silent!

How was the Roman empire divided?

With a pair of Caesars!

Who made King Arthur's round table?

Sir Cumference!

What happened when electricity was first discovered?

People got a nasty shock!

What do you call a dinosaur with no eyes?

Doyouthinkhesaurus!

Which figure in history ate the most?

Attila the Hungry!

Say this three times, quickly.

Cunning Cleopatra's clever scheming charmed Caesar!

Why was the ancient Egyptian mummy so tense?

He was always wound up!

Why were the ancient Egyptians so unhappy with their ruler?

Because he was being un-Pharaoh!

What was written on the knight's tomb?

"Rust in Peace!"

Which emperor should have stayed away from gunpowder?

Napoleon Blownapart!

What do you call a fortunate detective?

Sheerluck Holmes!

Why were the ancient Egyptians good at spying?

They kept things under wraps!

Which Russian leader was a big fan of fruit?

Peter the Grape!

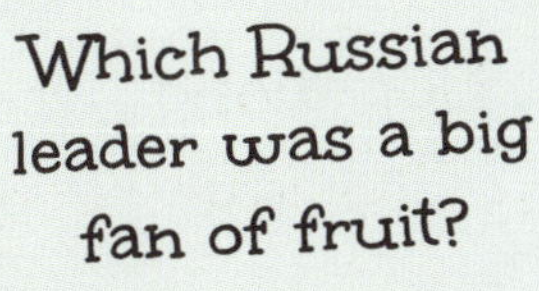

Say this three times, quickly.

Sly pirates spy pilots buying pies!

Which monarch had the worst skin?

Mary, Queen of Spots!

What is a forum?

Two-um plus two-um!

What do you call a frog who wants to be a cowboy?

Hop-along Cassidy!

Was Rome built in a day?

No, it was built in Italy!

Where did King Arthur's men get their training?

Knight school!

Why did the student miss the history exam?

He had the wrong date!

What was Robin Hood's mother called?

Mother Hood!

Knock, knock.

Who's there?

Genghis.

Genghis who?

Genghis must be the wrong house!

How did pharaohs get the best pyramids?

They asked for a tomb with a view!

Did you hear about the unembalmed ancient Egyptian discovery?

It sphinx!

Which famous explorer was good at sports?

Marco Polo!

Who invented matches?

Some bright spark!

Why did cavemen love to eat sloths?

They knew that fast food was bad for you!

Why did Robin Hood only steal from the rich?

Because the poor had nothing worth stealing!

Knock, knock.

Who's there?

Noah.

Noah who?

Noah good place to eat?

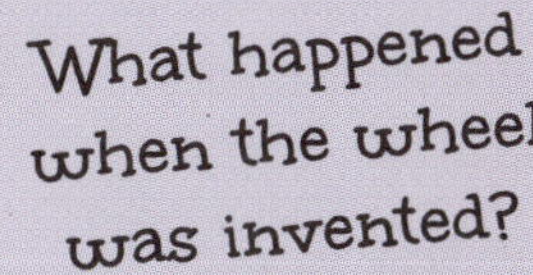

What happened when the wheel was invented?

It started a revolution!

Where was the Declaration of Independence signed?

At the bottom!

What did Henry VIII do whenever he burped?

He issued a Royal Pardon!

Why was King Arthur's table round?

So he couldn't be cornered!

Try saying this three times, quickly.

Upon the placid plains, the Pawnee ponies pranced!

What did Sir Lancelot's mother say to him at bedtime?

"Knight, knight!"

When in history did people have the nicest, smoothest clothes?

During the Iron Age!

Which fruit launched a thousand ships?

Melon of Troy!

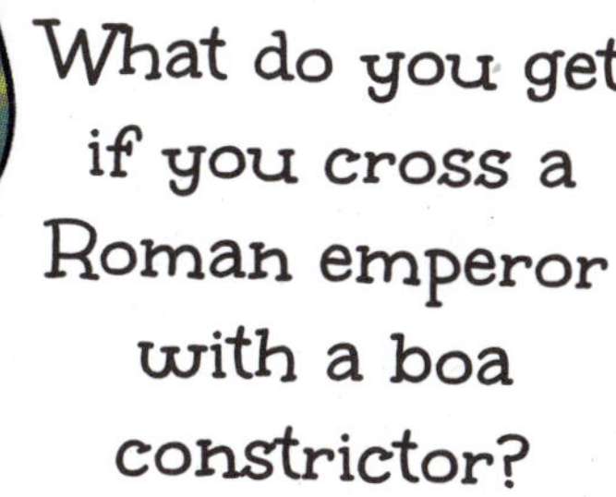

What do you get if you cross a Roman emperor with a boa constrictor?

Julius Squeezer!

What did the executioner shout to the line of prisoners?

"Necks, please!"

Knock, knock.

Who's there?

Jester.

Jester who?

Jester wondering if you were at home!

Did you hear about the T. rex that ate a firework?

It was dinomite!

What do you call a friendly pharaoh?

A chummy mummy!

What creature hunted in prehistoric oceans?

Jurassic shark!

What was Queen Victoria's most treasured item of clothing?

Her reign-coat!

Did you hear about the Shakespearean actor who fell through the floor?

It was a just a stage he was going through!

Why did cave people paint pictures of hippopotamuses?

They couldn't spell it!

How did cavemen make fire with two sticks?

They made sure one was a match!

Say this three times, quickly!

Robin Hood robbed the rich of their riches until King Rich's return!

Did you hear about the queen whose eldest son disobeyed her?

She was having a bad heir day!

What do you call a Roman emperor who has adventures?

An action Nero!

What was the prisoner doing in the medieval dungeon?

Just hanging!

Riddle me this!

I'm a sea where Egyptian mummies like to swim. What am I?

The Dead Sea.

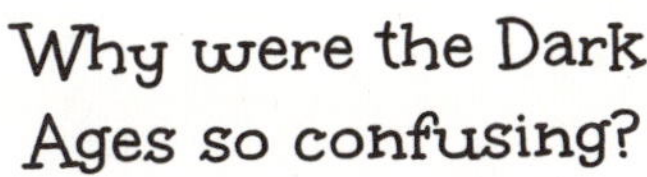

Why were the Dark Ages so confusing?

It was common to hear, "Good morning, good knight!"

What did Anne Boleyn's lady-in-waiting say on her wedding day?

"That man's not worth losing your head over!"

What sweet treat did cavemen like the best?

Spearmints!

Knock, knock.

Who's there?

Julius.

Julius who?

Julius, seize her! She took my wallet!

How did people tie their shoelaces in the Middle Ages?

With a longbow!

Why wouldn't the ancient Egyptian accept that his boat was sinking?

He was in de Nile!

Why did the cowboy choose his horse in broad daylight?

He didn't want a nightmare!

Why did the dragon spit out the court jester?

Because he tasted funny!

Say this three times, quickly.

On various voyages, vile Vikings revolted violently!

Why did the hangman's wife ask for a divorce?

Her husband was a pain in the neck!

Riddle me this.

People could catch me, but they couldn't throw me. What am I?

The plague.

What was T. rex's lucky number?

Eight!

What kind of dinosaur can you ride in a rodeo?

A Bronco-saurus!

Why is it no fun being an archeologist?

Your career is always in ruins!

What did the dragon say when it saw Sir Lancelot?

"Ugh, more canned food!"

Say this three times, quickly.

Sir Lancelot, please dance a lot! Thanks a lot.

How did Christopher Columbus get to college?

On a scholar-ship!

Nero: What time is it?

Servant: X past VII!

Which Roman emperor was the coolest?

Julius Freezer!

What loses its head in the morning but gets it back at night?

A pillow!

What kind of socks did pirates wear?

Arrr-gyle!

Which knight was King Arthur's best bodyguard?

Sir Curity!

What letters are like a Roman emperor?

The "Cs" are!

Who do archeologists invite to their parties?

Anyone they can dig up!

Which famous knight never won a battle?

Sir Endor!

Which knight was King Arthur's best lookout?

Sir Veillance!

Which animal discovered the Internet?

The beaver—it was the first to log on!

In which battle was Genghis Khan killed?

His last one!

What comes once in a minute, twice in a moment, but never in a thousand years?

The letter "m."

When did the Vikings make their raids?

During a plunder storm!

Did you hear about the mummy that lost its temper?

It flipped its lid!

Say this three times, quickly.

Caesar saw his sister sitting on a seesaw!

A Year of Laughter

Where do you find the best Easter egg jokes?

In a yolk book!

Why do skunks love Valentine's Day?

Because they're scent-imental!

Say this three times, quickly.

Peter Piper picked a pile of perfect pumpkins!

What sneaks around the kitchen on Christmas Eve?

Mince spies!

What did the slobbery dog say to her owner on Valentine's Day?

"I love you drooly, madly, deeply!"

How did Jack Frost break his leg at Christmas?

He fell off his icicle!

When does Christmas come before Thanksgiving?

In the dictionary!

How do you fix a jack-o'-lantern?

With a pumpkin patch!

Why was the Thanksgiving turkey under arrest?

For fowl play!

What monster plays tricks at Halloween?

Prankenstein!

What did the Easter bunny say about the horror film?

"That was hare-raising!"

Knock, knock.

Who's there?

Howl.

Howl who?

How-long till you open the door?

How do you win the Easter race?

By beating all the eggs!

Why was Santa's little helper shy?

He had low elf-esteem!

Why is it so cold at Christmas?

Because it's Decembrrrr!

When is a good time for Santa to come down the chimney?

Anytime!

How does the Easter bunny stay fit?

Eggs-ercise!

What should you wear to Thanksgiving dinner?

A har-vest!

Which of Santa's reindeers was always impolite?

RUDE-olph!!

Knock, Knock.

Who's there?

Mary.

Mary who?

Mary Christmas!

How do you start a Santa race?

On your marks, get set, ho, ho, ho!

Knock, knock.

Who's there?

Abby.

Abby who?

Abby New Year!

Did you hear the one about the broken egg?

It will crack you up!

What do you shout when Santa takes the roll call?

"Present!"

Did you hear the story about the giant pumpkin pie?

It's a hard one to swallow ...

Riddle me this!

If fruit comes from a fruit tree, where does turkey come from?

A poul-tree!

Why does Santa Claus enjoy being in the garden?

Because he likes to ho, ho, ho!

What do you get if you cross an apple with a Christmas tree?

A pineapple!

Why did the turkey want to join a band?

Because he already had the drumsticks!

Which ride do ghosts enjoy at Halloween?

The roller ghoster!

What birds write the most Christmas cards?

Pen-guins!

What happened when the snow woman got angry at the snowman?

She gave him the cold shoulder!

What do you get when you cross Santa Claus and Sherlock Holmes?

Santa Clues!

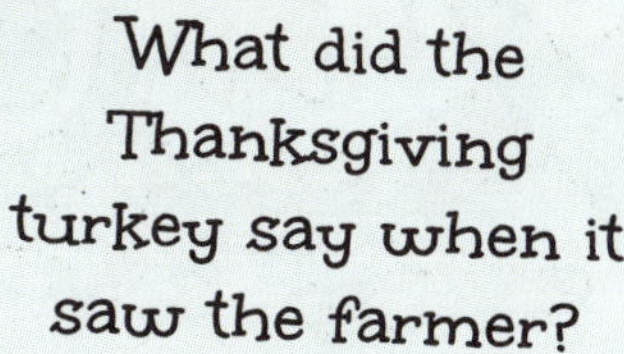

What do reindeer hang on their Christmas trees?

Horn-aments!

What did the Thanksgiving turkey say when it saw the farmer?

"Quack, quack!"

What did the magnet say to his girlfriend on Valentine's Day?

"You're very attractive!"

What did Adam say to his wife the night before Christmas?

"It's Christmas, Eve!"

What do snowmen sing to Santa on his birthday?

"Freeze a jolly good fellow!"

Say this three times, quickly!

Every Easter, Esther ate her eggs extremely eagerly!

What do birds do on Halloween?

They go trick-or-tweeting!

What is impossible to pass at Christmas?

The Three Wide Men!

What did the sheep say to the shepherds at Christmas?

"Seasons bleatings!"

What goes "Oh, oh, oh!" at Christmas?

Santa walking backward!

What do you call a line of Easter rabbits who've been waiting in the sun too long?

Hot cross bunnies!

What did the rabbits do after they got married?

They went on their bunny moon!

Why couldn't the elf work in Santa's toyshop?

He had tinsel-itis!

Riddle me this!

What always comes at the beginning of a parade?

The letter "p."

What do you call a female elf?

A shelf!

What kind of ball doesn't bounce?

A snowball!

How long should an elf's legs be?

Just long enough to reach the ground!

Riddle me this!

I have no hinge, door, or lid, but inside me, golden treasure is hidden. What am I?

An egg.

If Santa travels in a sleigh, what do his elves travel in?

A minivan!

How many elves does it take to change a light bulb?

Ten—one to change the bulb and nine to stand on each other's shoulders!

What song does a bull sing on Valentine's Day?

"When I fall in love, it will be for heifer!"

What kind of insect hates Christmas?

A bah humbug!

Where do the elves go to dance?

A snowball!

Say this three times, quickly.

Eleven elves licked eleven lemon lollipops!

Where do you find the most famous mistletoe?

Holly-wood!

What did Santa say when he first sighted America?

"Land ho, ho, ho!"

What kind of music does the Easter bunny listen to?
Hip-hop!
What do you call Santa when he's asleep?
Santa Pause!
How does the Easter bunny travel?
By hareplane!
Why was the chicken in a fluster?
Because she'd mislaid her eggs!

What does Jack Frost eat for breakfast?

Ice crispies!

Say this three times, quickly.

Seven slippery snowmen slide silently southward!

What kind of Easter eggs do aliens have?

Eggs-traterrestrial ones!

Did you hear about the magnets that broke up?

They were poles apart!

What is different about the Christmas alphabet?

It has no "L"!

What do you call it when chicks eat outdoors?

A peck-nic!

Did you hear about the lazy skeleton?

It was bone idle!

Why did the Easter bunny pull out of the marathon?

He was eggs-hausted!

Who visits mermaids at Easter?

The oyster bunny!

Which TV show does the Easter bunny like best?

Who Wants to Be a Million-Hare.

What do snowmen like to do after Christmas?

Chill out!

What do snowmen eat for breakfast?

Frosted flakes!

How can you send a letter to the Easter bunny?

By hare mail!

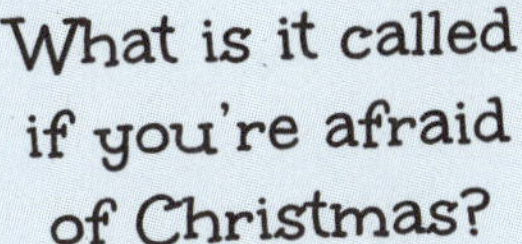

What is it called if you're afraid of Christmas?

Santa Claus-trophobia!

What did the python say to his girlfriend on Valentine's day?

"I've got a crush on you!"

What did the farmer give his wife on Valentine's Day?

Hogs and kisses!

What kind of flowers are no good for Valentine's Day?

Cauliflowers!

Knock, knock.

Who's there?

Owl.

Owl who?

Owl always love you, Valentine!

What did one snowman say to the other?

"Can you smell carrots?"

What do you call someone who steals gift wrap from the rich and gives it to the poor?

Ribbon Hood!

Did you hear about the stupid vampire?

He was a real sucker!

What did the gymnast say to her Valentine?
"I'm heels over head in love with you!"
Why is Santa so good at karate?
Because he has a black belt!
Who is never hungry at Christmas?
A turkey, because he's always stuffed!
What did the Cyclops write in his Valentine card?
"You're the one eye adore!"

What did the snail write in the Valentine's card?

"Be my Valen-slime!"

What do you call a snowman in summer?

Puddle!

What did Mrs. Claus say to Santa as she peered into the sky?

"Looks like rain deer!"

What kind of food is good for Valentine's Day?

A hearty meal!

What do Easter bunnies say to each other at Christmas?

"I wish you a Merry Christmas and a Hoppy New Year!"

What did the painter tell his girlfriend on Valentine's Day?

"I love you with all my art."

Who brings little crabs presents at Christmas?

Sandy Claws!

Riddle me this!

When Santa leaves the North Pole on Christmas Eve, in what direction does he travel?

South, because it is south in any direction from the North Pole.

What does a nearsighted ghost need?
Spook-tacles!
What swings through the trees and makes a great Christmas cake?
Tarzipan!
What did the chicken use when the hot cross buns were burning?
A fire eggs-tinguisher!
When do ghosts play tricks on each other?
April Ghoul's Day!

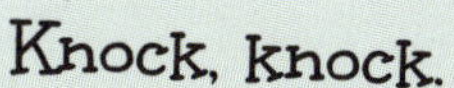

Knock, knock.

Who's there?

Hanna.

Hanna who?

Hanna partridge in a pear tree!

Why are graveyards so noisy?

Because of all the coffin!

What did the chicken gladiator shout at the Roman spectators?

Are you not HEN-tertained?!

What do you call two love birds?

Tweet hearts!

What is red and white and runs across the African plains?

A Santa-lope!

What carol is sung in the desert?

"O Cam-el Ye Faithful!"

What did the rabbit say to the policeman when he knocked on his door?

"I want to see your search warren!"

How did the sheep propose to his girlfriend?

"Will ewe be my wife?"

What's the best kind of Christmas present?

A broken drum, because you just can't beat it!

What do ghosts name their teddy bears?

Winnie-the-Boo!

What always comes at the end of Christmas dinner?

The letter "r."

Knock, knock.

Who's there?

Howard.

Howard who?

Howard you like to be my Valentine?

Who has fangs and webbed feet?

Count Quackula!

How do you upset a reindeer?

Make an off-the-hoof remark!

What do ghouls put on their bagels?

Scream cheese!

Which car do rabbits like best?

Any kind, as long as it's a hutchback!

Knock, knock.

Who's there?

Harvey.

Harvey who?

Harvey happy Easter!

How do you catch the Easter bunny?

Hide in the bushes, and make a noise like a carrot!

What did one Easter egg say to the other?

"Heard any good yolks recently?"

Why did Santa get a parking ticket?

He left his sleigh in a snow-parking zone!

Who gives presents to baby sharks?

Santa Jaws!

What carol does Tarzan sing at Christmas?

"Jungle Bells!"

What do snowmen wear on their heads?

Snowcaps!

What do you call a bunch of rabbits marching backward?

A receding hareline!

What do you call a Christmas tree with a really big nose?

Pine-occchio!

Why did the tortoises get married?

Because they were turtle-y in love!

Who is Jack Frost's best-loved aunt?

Aunt Arctica!

Why did Rudolph do so well at school?

Because he nose a lot and is very bright!

Where does Easter come before Valentine's Day?

In the dictionary!

How does the Easter bunny travel home?

With United Hareways!

How does Good King Wenceslas like his pizza?

Deep-pan, crisp, and even!

Say this three times, quickly.

How many deer would a reindeer rain, if a reindeer could rain deer?

What do angry rodents send each other at Christmas?

Cross-mouse cards!